IN TIMES OF SHAKING

Guideposts from the Book of Hebrews

IN TIMES OF SHAKING

GUIDEPOSTS FROM THE BOOK OF HEBREWS

Stephen Kaung

Christian Fellowship Publishers, Inc.
New York

Paperback ISBN: 978-1-68062-203-4
eBook ISBN: 978-1-68062-204-1

Available from the Publishers at:

11515 Allecingie Parkway
Richmond, Virginia 23235
www.c-f-p.com

Printed in the United States of America

Preface

We are living today in a time of great shaking. Not only are earthly things being shaken, but even spiritual things are being shaken. This shaking must take place in order that that which can be shaken will be removed, so that that which cannot be shaken may remain. Anything that can be shaken shall be removed because God has given us a kingdom that cannot be shaken, and He wants us to inherit that kingdom.

In such a time as this, the book of Hebrews has something to say to us because our situation is very similar to the situation facing the Hebrew believers in the first century. How will God's people be kept from being shaken away? How will they be kept pure and blameless until the day of Christ? Brother Kaung elaborates on three phrases from the book of Hebrews that are like guideposts for Christians in order to be kept in these days: Consider Jesus, within the veil, and outside the camp.

Therefore, let us …

Contents

Note

The messages contained in this book were spoken by Stephen Kaung before a group of believers in Richmond, Virginia, in the months of January and April 1983.

Unless otherwise indicated,
Scripture quotations are from the
New Translation by J. N. Darby

1—Consider Jesus

Hebrews 12:25-29—See that ye refuse not him that speaks, For if those did not escape who had refused him who uttered the oracles on earth, much more we who turn away from Him who does so from heaven: whose voice then shook the earth; but now he has promised, saying, Yet once will I shake not only the earth, but also the heaven, but this, Yet once, signifies the removing of what is shaken, as being made that what is not shaken may remain. Wherefore, let us receiving a kingdom not to be shaken, have grace by which let us serve God, acceptably with reverence and fear. For also our God is a consuming fire.

Hebrews 3:1—Wherefore, holy brethren, partakers of the heavenly calling, consider the Apostle and High Priest of our confession, Jesus.

The book of Hebrews was written before AD 70, before the destruction of Jerusalem and its temple. It was written to the Hebrew believers, that is, those Jews who believed in the Lord Jesus in the first century, as a preparation for the catastrophe that was going to fall upon that nation. In other words, God was preparing His people for what was coming to them very soon.

Once, God shook the earth as He gave the oracles to the children of Israel. We know that happened at Mount Sinai. When God gave the Law to the children of Israel, God descended upon the mountain in fire, and the whole mountain shook. It was a terrible sight, and even Moses proclaimed that he was in trembling and fear. But that was not to be compared with what God has promised: that, "Yet once," God will not only shake the earth, but He will also shake the heaven. This quotation is originally from the book of Haggai "…yet once, … I [God] will shake the heavens and the earth …" (2:6), and it will be finally and literally fulfilled at the coming of our Lord Jesus as He establishes His kingdom upon this earth. If you want to know how it will be fulfilled, you can read the book of Revelation. There you will find how this prophecy will be finally and literally fulfilled.

But we know this prophecy is partially and spiritually fulfilled at the destruction of Jerusalem and its temple. Why? Because as we read the context of the book of Hebrews, we find that this is written to the Hebrew believers to prepare them for the great shaking that was coming to them in AD 70.

Therefore, we know that this prophecy can be partially and spiritually applied even to that time. I believe it was John Owen, that great Puritan theologian, who mentioned that this can refer to the worship of the Mosaic order as the heavenly things. God will shake the heaven and the earth. The heaven refers to the Mosaic worship, and the earth refers to the political state of that nation at the time of AD 70.

To the Jews at that time, Jerusalem and the temple were considered heavenly things. Why? Because Jerusalem was a city that was chosen by God Himself. In Deuteronomy chapter 12, God said that after they entered into the land of promise, He would choose a place to put His name there. And all the children of Israel must go to that place to offer their sacrifices. So, Jerusalem was chosen by God. Psalm 132 says that the Lord has chosen Zion; He has desired it for His habitation.

Jerusalem, as well as the temple in Jerusalem, were heavenly things to the Jews, not just earthly things. We remember how David, in his great love for God, desired to build God a temple. Even though God did not allow him to build that temple because he was a man of war, God was pleased with that idea. And God promised that his son Solomon would build that temple. So both Jerusalem and its temple were always considered by the Jews as things of heaven, things that came from God.

However, God said that one day He would shake not only the earth, but He would also shake the heaven. Not only earthly things will be shaken, but even heavenly things will also be shaken. That is, Jerusalem and its temple will all be destroyed. Now, why is it so? The reason was that both Jerusalem and its temple actually were shadows. They were to prepare the way for the substance—Christ Jesus. All these things were set until the time when the Lord would come, and then the shadows would pass away, for the substance had finally arrived.

God gave the Jewish people Jerusalem, a place of worship. God gave them the temple where they could enter and worship God, yet these were but preparations. They were not the eternal substance. They were imposed until the time of the coming of Christ. Now that Christ had come, the substance had arrived, but these Jews who believed in the Lord Jesus still clung to the shadows. On the one hand, they believed in the Lord Jesus; on the other hand, they still held on to Moses. On the one hand, they gathered together to break bread on the Lord's day, but on the

Sabbath, they went into the synagogues to worship God. So, in those days, these Hebrew believers were actually holding on to both Christ and to Moses, both to the substance and to the shadow, to the extent that the shadow became a hindrance to their entering into the fullness of Christ. In view of that, God was going to do something to free these Hebrew believers from the bondage of Judaism into the liberty of Christ. That is the reason why this book was written—to prepare them. When Jerusalem and the temple were destroyed, these believers would know what God intended to do so that they would not be under a kind of despair, but instead they would be freed from all bondages and enter into the full liberty of Christ. So this is the background of the book of Hebrews.

We do feel that this book is very relevant to our days. In other words, we feel that this book has something to say to us today because our situation is very similar to the situation of the Hebrew believers in the first century. We are also living in a day of great shaking. I believe everybody knows that this is not something in the future, but actually, we today are already in the time of great shaking. Not only is the earth being shaken, but even the heaven is also being shaken. When we look around us, whether we look at the international situation, the national situation, the political situation, the economic situation, or the moral situation, we find that everything around us seems to be greatly shaken. Those standards that were set up long ago are no longer honored. We find everything around us just crumbles down. We are in the time of great shaking.

Recently, when I was in Hong Kong, I told the brethren: Of all things upon this earth, we find that nothing is real but one, and that is *real estate*. We think that is real. Everything will change. Currency will change, but we think that real estate is real. But this time, when I was in Hong Kong, real estate is no longer real because of the possibility that Communist China will take over Hong Kong in 15 years, or maybe earlier than that. And when this news began to come out, real estate just became unreal.[1] Nothing on this earth is real. The whole earth is being shaken. There is nothing that we can hold on to as if it will last. No, everything upon the earth is being shaken.

But dear brothers and sisters, not only the earth is being shaken, even the heaven is being shaken. Not

---

[1] When this ministry was given, Hong Kong was scheduled to revert from British rule back to Chinese rule, which happened in 1997.

literally—one day it will happen—but spiritually, whatever we call heavenly things, are now being greatly challenged and greatly tested. We find great shaking everywhere, not only without, but even within. Today, within Christianity, even in theological seminaries, we find all these modern ideas are coming out, such as "God is dead," or whatever it may be. Our very faith is being tested within. And our faith is being tested without as well. We find persecutions over a great part of this world. If people are the Lord's, even if they acknowledge themselves as believers, it is considered as a crime. They will be forced to deny their faith to see whether their faith is real or whether it is unreal.

Do you remember what our Lord Jesus said? "When the Son of Man comes, will He find faith on the earth?" (see Luke 18:8). Because of the lawlessness that prevails upon the earth, the love of many shall grow cold. Dear brothers and sisters, you find even our faith, our love, everything that we consider as heavenly things are now being tested and contested. We live in a time of great shaking. Now, when the world notices what they are going through today and what is coming to them, of course, they are filled with fear. But the Bible says, "When you see these things coming, lift up your heads, because your redemption draws near" (see Luke 21:28).

I do believe that we are in a time of great shaking, but we need to thank God for the great shaking, because God wants us to inherit the kingdom that cannot be shaken. I think it is but right for us to understand this, because there are many things that we hold tightly that may be shaken off. Why? Because they are shadows; they are not the reality. And it is good for us to see that whatever is not real will be shaken off, that we may inherit that which is eternal.

So, we feel that today we are in a day of great shaking. Why does God allow these things to happen to us? It is because Christianity today has become so Judaized that instead of being a living faith, a revelation from above, it has become an institution, a religion, just like the Jewish faith. In the beginning, it was revelation. In the beginning, it was a living faith, but gradually it has become Judaism, an "ism," a religion. And Christianity is the same. In the beginning, it is a revelation. In the beginning, it is a living faith, but today it has become so Judaized that it has become an institution; it has become a religion. In view of the soon coming of our Lord Jesus, He has to deliver us from that which is unreal to that which is real. He has to deliver us from that which is outward appearance into that which is the inward reality. I believe it is for this reason that God allows such great shaking around the world today among His own people.

The Elements of Judaism

Probably a word should be said about Judaism. What is Judaism? Judaism was formed by five elements.

Number one: a definite place of worship. In Judaism, worship was limited to one place, and that was Jerusalem. Every year, three times a year, all the males of the Jewish people must travel to Jerusalem to worship God. They were not allowed to offer sacrifices anywhere else in the world, but only in Jerusalem in the temple; that is the one place of worship.

Number two: In Judaism, they have a set of laws. God gave them the Ten Commandments, and with the Ten Commandments, all the statutes and the ordinances and the precepts. They have a set of laws to govern them.

Number three: They have an intermediatory class—the Levites, the priests—because the people were not allowed to worship God directly. They have to worship God through that intermediatory class called the priesthood, the Levites.

Number four: They have a group of earthly promises. If you read the Old Testament, God promised the Jewish people He would bless them. That is, if they love and fear God and keep His covenant and commandments, then God would bless them with many children. He would bless their cattle and their sheep, and He would give them a full basket. Now, all these blessings are earthly and material blessings. That is Judaism.

Now, aside from these four things, what really makes it Judaism is actually **number five:** the traditions of the fathers. God gave the children of Israel the Law, but how was the Law to be interpreted? How was the Law to be applied to the details of daily life? Through the years, great rabbis, great teachers came up, and they began to interpret and explain the Law of God. They began to apply the Law of God to the details of life. Then, another generation—more teachers, rabbis, came out—and instead of interpreting the Law of God, they began to interpret the interpretation of the rabbis before them. And then another generation came, and great teachers arrived. They came to interpret the interpretation of the interpretation of the great teachers of the Law of God. So throughout the years, gradually, a great pile of traditions accumulated called the "traditions of the fathers." The traditions of the fathers became so strong that even at the time of our Lord Jesus, the Lord said, "You keep the traditions of the fathers, and you violate the Law of God." In other words, the commandment of God was buried and hidden under a pile of traditions. That is how the living faith among the Jews became a religion, an institutional religion, became Judaism. Now, brothers and sisters, you can see very clearly how Christianity today has been completely Judaized.

Number One: A Definite Place of Worship

When we think of worship, someone will say, "Let's go to church." Now, what do you mean by church? Probably what you mean by church is a building, maybe built of brick, or maybe built of stone, or if you are in some uncivilized country, maybe made of mud. But anyway, we say that we go to the place of worship, that is, we mean we go to a definite place—a building—and that building is called the place of worship.

When we talk of worship, we think of Sunday because Sunday is the day of worship. In other words, to many believers today, worship is a matter of place and time. There is a definite place called the place of worship, and there is a certain time called the time of worship. In the bulletin, you will find *worship* is Sunday morning from 10 o'clock to 11 o'clock. Now, what is worship? Actually, when you go there, you find you are being entertained; it is not that God is worshiped. And if you are not well-entertained, you probably have to go to another place of worship to be better entertained. Another thing you find, even with lots of so-called believers, is that they go to worship only once a year on Christmas Day, or if they are better, maybe twice a year on Easter, too.

Anyway, in Christianity today, worship is restricted to place and time. But do you remember our Lord's conversation with the Samaritan woman in John chapter four? When the conscience of the Samaritan woman was awakened by the Lord, she began to ask about this matter of worship. So she inquired of the Lord and said, "We Samaritans worship on this mountain (that is, Mount Gerizim), but you Jews worship in Jerusalem, in the temple. Which is correct? Where should we worship?" And you remember the Lord said, "Woman, the time is coming, and now is, that you do not worship either in Mount Gerizim or in Jerusalem in the temple. But God is a Spirit and is seeking for true worshipers, those who worship Him in spirit and in truth."

Dear brothers and sisters, what is our faith? Our faith is that we worship the Father in spirit and in truth. It is no longer to be limited to a place or to a time. In other words, we worship Him all the time; we worship Him everywhere. We worship Him in spirit and in truth. Now, it is true that sometimes we come together to worship Him, but that does not mean that when we are alone, we do not need to worship Him. It is no longer a matter of place or time; it is spirit and truth. But unfortunately, to many Christians today, worship is still a matter of time and space. It is as if we worship God on Sunday, but from Monday to Saturday it is our time. We can do whatever we like. We can worship mammon if we want to, but on Sunday, we come to worship God. However, the Bible says a man cannot serve two masters. We cannot serve God and serve mammon. Christianity has been Judaized. It has become a religion instead of a living faith.

Number Two: A Set of Laws

In Judaism, we find a set of laws. God gave the Ten Commandments and all the precepts, the ordinances, and the statutes. Now, do we have these in Christianity? Does God give us eleven commandments? Is our life as a Christian to be governed by rules and regulations? If we read the Bible, we find with us, there is only one law, and that is the law of the Spirit of life. In other words, God has put His Holy Spirit in us, and the Spirit of life is the law that governs our living. But today, how many believers are still governed by the rules and regulations of the church that they belong to? Instead of being ruled by the Spirit of God within, they still walk an outward way of rules and regulations, and that is Judaized Christianity.

Number Three: An Intermediatory Class

In Judaism, you will find an intermediatory class called the priesthood. But in the New Testament, as we come to the Lord, we are all living stones being built up together a spiritual house, a holy priesthood (see I Peter 2:5). In other words, in the New Covenant, there is the universal priesthood of believers. Every believer is a priest. We do not have an intermediatory class between us and God. Our Lord Jesus is the only mediator between us and God. Today, through our Lord Jesus, we can come directly to God. We can worship Him and serve Him because all of us believers are priests.

But dear brothers and sisters, is this true in Christianity? Today, in Christianity, there is still the so-called sacred class, the clergy, and the laity. In other words, you are the laymen, and all that the laymen are required to do is pay their dues and attend a Sunday meeting. Then all the spiritual works are being monopolized by a class of sacred people called the clergy. They are set apart to do all the things for you. This is not living faith. This is a religion. This is Judaistic Christianity.

Number Four: A Group of Earthly Promises

In Judaism, there is a group of promises, but all these promises were earthly and physical and material, because the children of Israel are God's earthly people. But we, who are the Lord's today, are God's heavenly people. Dear brothers and sisters, do you notice in the Bible, in the New Testament, that God has blessed us with every spiritual blessing in the heavenlies, in Christ Jesus? (see Ephesians 1:3). God has blessed us with every spiritual blessing in the heavenlies, in Christ Jesus. Why? Because we are God's heavenly people.

So, God's blessings to us today are heavenly and spiritual. Now, that does not mean that God does not supply us with our daily bread. Certainly, He still takes care of our physical needs; but remember that the blessings that God has promised to His church are spiritual and heavenly.

But today, does it sometimes confuse you when you hear about what is very popular in this country, called "the prosperity gospel"? In other words, if you believe in the Lord Jesus, then God will prosper you financially, prosper you materially. You do not need to drive a Chevrolet; you can drive a Cadillac. Now, is that not Judaized Christianity?

Number Five: The Traditions of the Fathers

In the beginning, Christianity was a revelation from above. The heavenly Father revealed His Son in us. It is a living faith. But today, we find there is very little revelation known among God's people, but there is a lot of tradition. In other words, the way that we act, the way that we behave: Why do we do things this way? Why do we gather this way? Whatever is connected with so-called religious life is actually based on tradition. It is because the fathers have been doing that, the grandfathers have been doing that. You do not have a living revelation from God. Everything is based on tradition, not on revelation.

Now, we do not mean that today we can have new revelation extra to the Bible; of course not. All the revelations of God are contained in the Bible. We cannot have new revelation extra to the Bible, but still, whatever is revealed in the Bible must be revealed to us, too. That is revelation. Then it will be real. The word of God, the *logos* of God, has to become *rhema* to us; it has to become a living life to us. But today, unfortunately, many believers live on traditions. They do not have that revelation from above. It is for this reason that Christianity today has been totally Judaized. Instead of giving us Christ, it has become a substitute for Christ, and God is very jealous about it.

Do you remember that story on the Mount of Transfiguration? There, our Lord Jesus took His three disciples to that Mount, and He was transfigured. It was a preview of the kingdom that cannot be shaken. Moses and Elijah appeared, and they talked with our Lord Jesus about His exit, how He will leave the world. And you remember how Peter, as if he just awoke from his slumber and he saw that scene. It was so wonderful. So he blurted out and said, "It is good to be here. Let us make three tabernacles, one for you Lord, one for Moses, and one for Elijah." He thought he was being very generous because he and John and James were just sleeping in the open air. But the moment he said that, God took away Moses and took away Elijah, and a bright cloud covered them, and they heard the voice: "This is my beloved Son. Hear Him." When they opened their eyes, they saw no one but Jesus only. Why? It is because God is very jealous for His Son. When Peter tried to put Moses and Elijah on the same footing as the Lord Jesus, God said, "No, you cannot do that." Not only can you not substitute Moses for Christ, or Elijah for Christ, you cannot even put Moses and Elijah on the same footing as Christ. God took away Moses, He discharged Elijah because God said, "This is My beloved Son. Hear Him" (see Matthew 17).

God's Great Shaking

Dear brothers and sisters, the same jealous God is jealous for His Son today. And I believe it is for this reason, at least this is one of the reasons, why God is shaking the heaven and shaking the earth today. God wants to free us from Christianity as a religion, into the fullness of Christ. Christianity has become a substitute for Christ today. Christianity has deceived us into thinking that we have Christ. But dear brothers and sisters, we need to wake up and see that all things that are considered as Christianity are being shaken today, and we will not have Christianity anymore.

There are many places in the world where you cannot find a definite place of worship; you cannot go to a place called the place of worship. There are many places in the world where there cannot be a fixed time of worship. If you want to worship God, you have to worship Him in spirit and in truth. Whatever is external, whatever is an "ism," and whatever is a religion will have to go. It will no longer exist because God wants us to have the reality.

We are in a day when rules and regulations will not hold anymore. It is the Spirit of God within us, and He never leaves us nor forsakes us.

We are living in a day when God will take away all those people whom we depend upon, as if our faith in God depends upon these people, but God will take them away. We have to see that we have to worship God and serve Him directly.

We are living in a time when even our properties, everything will be taken away from us, even our life will be in jeopardy. Will we still believe God? Will our faith still be vibrant and living?

We are living in a day when traditions will all crumble down. They will not be able to support us unless we have revelation from above, and that will keep us through any trials and persecution.

Brothers and sisters, we believe that God allows this great shaking to happen to the world today for our good, and it is time for us to wake up and let all these things that can be shaken, be shaken away. Do not cling on to these things. Let all these things go, because sooner or later, they will go and be shaken off.

Oh, how we thank God that anything that is made, anything that belongs to the old creation, anything that belongs to man, will be shaken away, only that which is God, which is of Christ, will remain forever. So it is time for us to understand what is going on in this world today, that we may not despair, but instead we may press on into that which God has called us.

Now brothers and sisters, as we are in this time of great shaking, what should we do? When we are in great shaking, it is a time for us to consider. Is it not now time for us to consider? Surely, it is. But what are we to consider?

Consider Jesus

> Wherefore, holy brethren, partakers of [the] heavenly calling, consider the Apostle and High Priest of our confession, Jesus (Hebrews 3:1).

Some people consider and say, "Well, probably there will be nuclear war coming, so flee to the desert. If we live in a city, probably we will be hit. But if we live in a faraway desert, then we can be saved." Other people say, "Great famine will be coming. What will you do? Consider. Store food." And it becomes a great big business. Dehydrated food becomes a big business. But the thing is, if you have food and nobody else has, are you able to eat it? Then you say, "Well, buy guns to protect yourself, to protect your food." Brothers and sisters, not only the worldly people, but even Christians are considering all these things. Isn't that foolish?

What should we consider? The Bible tells us "consider." Yes, we need to consider, but what should we consider? We should consider not all these things, but we should consider one Person, Jesus. This is a time that we should consider Jesus, the Apostle and the High Priest of our confession. There is nothing that can save us through this great shaking, but the Lord Jesus … consider Jesus.

Now, who is this Jesus that we must consider? He is the Apostle and the High Priest of our confession.

The Apostle of Our Confession

Our Lord Jesus is the Apostle of our confession. What does it mean? An apostle means one who is being sent, who is sent on a mission. Our Lord Jesus is the Apostle of our confession. He is sent by God into this world as an apostle to represent God. No one has ever seen the Father, but the Son has declared Him. The Lord Jesus said, "If you see Me, you see My Father." Why? Because He is the Apostle of God. God has sent Him into this world to represent Him. And what a perfect representation He is! He has not misrepresented God in any way. He has represented God perfectly.

By seeing the Lord Jesus, we see God the Father. He is the Apostle of God. He was sent on a mission to fulfill the work of redemption. And here we will find our Lord Jesus, as He was on the cross before He died, He said, "It is finished." What is finished? His mission is fulfilled; it is accomplished. What God has sent Him to accomplish has been accomplished. He has died for us. He has fulfilled the work of redemption. And not only that, but the Bible says He is risen from the dead, and He has now entered into heaven as our Leader. In other words, He has opened a way for us to heaven.

Dear brothers and sisters, consider our Lord Jesus as the Apostle of our confession, and in considering Him as the Apostle of our confession, what should we do? It is very simple: hear Him. He is the Apostle of God, therefore, hear Him. Listen to Him. What He says to us is true. What He has done for us is true. What He has opened for us is true. Just hear Him. Believe in Him. Follow Him because He is the Apostle of our confession. Do not follow man. Do not hear what man says, but hear Him and follow Him. He is the Apostle of God.

The High Priest of Our Confession

But He is not only the Apostle of our confession, the Bible says He is also the High Priest of our confession. When He was on earth, He was the Apostle of our confession. Now He is in heaven. He is the High Priest of our confession. As Apostle, He represents God towards man, but as High Priest, He is representing us before God. Most of us know Him as the Apostle because we know what He did on earth. But probably many of us are not very well-acquainted with Him as our High Priest.

What is the Lord doing today in heaven? I often remember the story about an elderly sister when she wanted to be baptized. It was the custom of those days that she had to go through a kind of examination of her faith. So she was brought in before a group of elders sitting there. And of course, she was frightened, and they began to question her faith and ask her various questions. And one of the questions asked was: What is the Lord doing in heaven today? And this sister really did not know, so she answered and said, "The Lord is standing in heaven looking down upon the earth at me to find fault with me. That is what the Lord Jesus is doing today in heaven." Of course, we know that is not true.

Our Lord Jesus sits at the right hand of the Father. What does it mean by seated? It means that the work of redemption is done. If the work of redemption is not finished, then He cannot sit. He has to stand, but now, our Lord Jesus sits at the right hand of the Father. Why? Because on earth He has finished the work of redemption. It is finished. However, that does not mean He sits there and takes a nap because He has nothing to do; everything is done. Not at all! The Bible says that He sits at the right hand of God. He liveth forever making intercession for us, and He is able to save to the uttermost those who come to God through Him (see Hebrews 7:25).

Our Lord Jesus is very, very busy in heaven today, not because His work on earth is unfinished—it *is* finished—but because there is something more to be done. He is there representing you and me. Thank God for that! Brothers and sisters, do you know that if you do not know Christ as the Apostle, you will never be saved? Do you know that if you do not know Christ as your High Priest, you can never live a Christian life? Why is it that so many believers today, they believe in the Lord Jesus, they are saved, and yet they are struggling through their Christian life? Why? It is because they do not know the Lord Jesus as their High Priest.

Remember, you have Christ Jesus representing you in the very presence of God the Father. He is there for you, representing you. He is there making intercession for you. You may not know how to pray for yourself, but He knows. Even when you are not praying, He is praying for you. And when your prayer is weak, He adds His prayer to your prayer. Do you not know that He is there able to save you to the uttermost?

What is meant by the High Priest? It means, through Him, you are able to enter and to live in the very presence of God and to please God. By yourself, you cannot. Lots of believers today are trying to live by themselves, to live the life of Christ by themselves. They try to live up to a standard. They want to be good Christians, but it is all self-effort. They mean well, and they really put their whole being into it. But the more they try, the more they find it is impossible. You cannot do that. But do you know you have a High Priest, One who is now in heaven, but who has once come to this earth? He is sympathetic with you, not because He is strong, therefore He is not sympathetic. He is sympathetic with you because He was tempted in all things, just like you are, but without sin. He is not only able to sympathize with you, He is able to support you. He is able to carry you through. He is your High Priest.

Brothers and sisters, depend on Him. It is through Him and by Him. That is something we need to learn. We cannot live as a Christian if we do not live by Him, if we do not depend on Him. Oh, come to Him! Look to Him. He is our High Priest. Cry to Him. Approach Him with boldness, and you will find mercy. You will receive grace for your seasonable help. Brothers and sisters, consider Him. Consider Jesus, your High Priest.

What do we mean by knowing Him as your High Priest? Now, sometimes we think that He is our High Priest. There He sits in heaven, far, far from us, and there He is praying for us. And is that all He does, just pray for us? Well, you do not know the power of prayer. As He prays for us, do you know what happens? As He prays for us, the Holy Spirit within us begins to work. You do not know Christ as the High Priest separated from the ministry of the Holy Spirit. As a matter of fact, His being High Priest is connected with the ministry of the Holy Spirit because when He ascended up on high, God has anointed Him. In Psalm 133, you will find the oil comes down from Aaron's head—that is the high priest—and the ointment, the oil, began to flow down through the whole body, even to the hem of the skirt.

So, His being High Priest is closely related with the ministry of the Holy Spirit in us. As our Lord Jesus prays, He prays according to God. Sometimes we pray, we do not know what we pray for. We pray amiss. But when He prays, He prays according to God, and God hears Him, and the Holy Spirit begins to work in our lives.

Dear brothers and sisters, the working of the Holy Spirit in our lives today is the result of the high priestly function of our Lord Jesus. The Holy Spirit is working in us. As He is working in us, He is bringing us into Christ.

Our Lord Jesus is a High Priest according to the order of Melchizedek. He is that High Priest in the power of an indissoluble life, in the power of eternal life, that is the way He is our High Priest. And dear brothers and sisters, we can experience this. How? We can experience the power of the eternal life within us. Oh, thank God, there is His life in us! And this life is eternal life, indissoluble life. This life is a conquering life. This life is a glorious life. This life is a life that has been tested and has been proven. This life is in us, and we experience this life, the power of this life in us, through the Holy Spirit. And that is the work of our Lord Jesus, as our High Priest. He is representing us before God, and through His prayer and through the working of the Holy Spirit, He is bringing us into maturity. He is bringing us into glory.

The Kingdom that Cannot be Shaken

Everything is shaking around us, but if it is Christ, it is unshakable. What is the kingdom that we are to inherit? What is the kingdom? On the Mount of Transfiguration, you can see the principle of the kingdom—the Son, Jesus Christ. He is the principle of the kingdom. He *is* the kingdom, and that kingdom cannot be shaken. So, if you find something being shaken off from you, do not worry about it. If it can be shaken, it will be shaken sooner or later, and it is much better if it is sooner that we be not deceived in any way.

But thank God, dear brothers and sisters, we know there is something in us that cannot be shaken. God has given us Christ. He is the kingdom that cannot be shaken. Oh, that we may enter into that kingdom abundantly. Do not enter into that kingdom as one barely saved, but as Peter says, "Let us enter into the kingdom abundantly, richly" (see II Peter 1:11). And what does that mean? It means with much of Christ. Oh, that we may know Him! Let us consider Him. Let us think about Him, meditate on Him, commune with Him, ask Him to fill us, because He is the only One that cannot be shaken, and thank God He is ours!

2—Within the Veil

Hebrews 12:25-29—See that ye refuse not him that speaks. For if those did not escape who had refused him who uttered the oracles on earth, much more we who turn away from him who does so from heaven: whose voice then shook the earth; but now he has promised, saying, Yet once will I shake not only the earth, but also the heaven. But this, Yet once, signifies the removing of what is shaken as being made that what is not shaken may remain. Wherefore let us, receiving a kingdom not to be shaken, have grace, by which let us serve God acceptably with reverence and fear. For also our God is a consuming fire.

Hebrews 6:17-20—Wherein God, willing to shew more abundantly to the heirs of the promise, the unchangeableness of his purpose, intervened by an oath, that by two unchangeable things, in which it was impossible that God should lie, we might have a strong encouragement, who have fled for refuge to lay hold on the hope set before us, which we have as anchor of the soul, both secure and firm, and entering into that within the veil, where Jesus

> is entered as forerunner for us, become for ever a high priest according to the order of Melchizedek.
> Hebrews 10:19-25—Having therefore, brethren, boldness for entering into the holy of holies by the blood of Jesus, the new and living way which he has dedicated for us through the veil, that is, his flesh, and having a great priest over the house of God, let us approach with a true heart, in full assurance of faith, sprinkled as to our hearts from the wicked conscience, and washed as to our body with pure water. Let us hold fast the confession of the hope unwavering, (for he is faithful who has promised;) and let us consider one another for provoking to love and good works; not forsaking the assembling of ourselves together, as the custom is with some; but encouraging one another, and by so much the more as ye see the day drawing near.

This letter to the Hebrews was written to the Hebrews who turned to be Christians in the first century. The Spirit of God gave this letter to them to prepare them for the coming catastrophe. God was going to shake, not only the earth, but also the heaven. That is to say, God is not only going to shake earthly things, secular things, but He is also going to shake heavenly or spiritual things.

God was going to do such shaking at that time because He wanted to shake loose those Hebrews who became Christians from the bondage of Judaism into the liberty of Christ. By the destruction of Jerusalem and the destruction of the holy temple in Jerusalem, the Hebrews who became Christians in the first century, were finally broken loose from Moses into Christ.

We believe that this book is very relevant for us today. It is not only relevant, but it is urgent. Why? Because we are living in a time that God is shaking not only the earth but also the heaven. Christianity has become so Judaized that God wants to shake His people out of Christianity into Christ.

Christianity is like a shadow that should introduce us to the substance that is Christ. But instead of that, Christianity today has become a substitute for Christ, and God is very jealous for His Son. God will not allow anything to compare, but also not to compete with His Son. That is why today we find everything around us is being shaken; not only the whole world is in a great shaking, but even the Christian world is in great shaking. We find that even in our personal spiritual experience, we are under great shaking. Why? Because it is the will of God that that which can be removed shall be removed. Only that which cannot be removed shall remain because it is God's will for us to inherit the kingdom that cannot be shaken.

During this period of shaking, God's word to His people is: "Consider Jesus, the Apostle and the High Priest of our confession." How will God keep His people during this time of great shaking from being shaken away and keep them pure and blameless until the day of Christ? You notice that in this book of Hebrews, there are two phrases which are very catching: "within the veil," and "outside the camp." These two phrases are guideposts for God's people today to be kept through the great shaking and to inherit the kingdom that cannot be shaken. For this time, we would like to just focus our attention on this matter of *within the veil.*

The Veil in the Tabernacle

I think probably a little history is needed. You know, after God redeemed His children of Israel, and delivered them out of Egypt, He took them through the Red Sea to the foot of Mount Sinai. There God gave them the Ten Commandments, the Law. Actually, the giving of the Law was not the purpose of

God concerning His people. The giving of the Law was just a preparation or an introduction; the purpose of God with His people was revealed by God commanding Moses to build Him a tabernacle.

We must remember that it is not God's purpose to put us under the Law that we may be condemned. It is God's purpose that He may dwell among His people, and in order that He may dwell among His people, He had to give them the commandments to let them know themselves, that they would appreciate Him and His grace. So, the purpose of God is shown in the tabernacle. God told Moses to build Him a sanctuary, a tabernacle, that He may dwell among His people (see Exodus 25:8). We know that this is God's eternal thought. Even before He created mankind, God had this thought in Him. He wanted to dwell among mankind. How was He to do that? How was He to dwell among the children of Israel, whom He had just delivered out of Egypt? He would dwell among them by a tabernacle.

If you know something about the tabernacle, on the outside of the tabernacle was the outer court, and all the children of Israel could enter into this court. There, they could bring their sacrifices to God, and the priest would offer these sacrifices on the brazen altar.

Then, within the outer court there was the holy place—the place where the priests could enter. The children of Israel could not enter into the holy place, only the priests—those whom God had set apart for His service—could enter into the holy place. There, they would light the golden lamp-stand, they would put shewbread on the table of shewbread, and they would burn incense on the golden altar of incense.

Behind the holy place, there was the holiest of all. That was where the presence of God dwelt. There was the ark of the covenant, and above the ark, as the cover of the ark, was the mercy seat. And God's glory dwelt on the mercy seat between the two cherubim.

Between the holy place and the holiest of all, there was a very heavy veil. We are told that even if you were to put two oxen or two horses on opposite sides and try to pull the veil, you could not rip it. It was a very heavy veil, and this veil separated the holy place and the holiest of all. No one could enter into the holiest of all. The children of Israel could not enter into the holiest of all, nor could the priests enter in, only the high priest. Once a year, on the Day of Atonement, he would enter behind the veil with blood and the smoke of incense to cover him. There he would make atonement for himself and for the nation of Israel, and after he did that, he quickly retreated.

You find that God wanted to dwell among His people. God wanted to have fellowship with His people. Yet, even though this was the desire of the Lord, it seems as if God said: "You cannot have fellowship with Me." God, on the one hand, called them to come to Him, yet on the other hand, He says, "Stay away, because I am holy."

The Bible says:

> Now these things being thus ordered, into the first tabernacle the priest enter at all times, accomplishing the services; but into the second, the high priest only, once a year, not without blood, which he offers for himself and for the errors of the people: the Holy Spirit shewing this, that the way to the holy of holies has not yet been made manifest, while, as yet the first tabernacle has its standing; the which is an image for the present time, according to which both gifts and sacrifices, unable to perfect as to conscience him that worshipped, are offered, consisting only of meats and drinks and divers washings, ordinances of flesh, imposed until the time of setting things right. But Christ being come ... (Hebrews 9:6-11a).

Here you find the tabernacle by which God dwelt among His people. Even though the people could come to the court to offer sacrifices, even though the priests could enter into the holy place to serve God, and yet, the way to the holy of holies has not yet been opened. The very fact that the high priest could only go in once a year proved that the way to the holiest of holies had not yet been opened. In other words, all these sacrifices, all these ordinances were but a shadow. They were there serving as a type, a shadow. They would be there until the time of setting things right. And the time of setting things right is the time when Christ is come.

In Exodus chapter 26, you find how the veil was made. A veil was to be made to be put between the holy place and the holiest of all. And this veil was made of blue, purple, scarlet, and of twined byssus (that is linen), and embroidered over it with artistic work of cherubim. This veil was to separate the holiest of all from the holy place and from the court.

The Veil—the Life of Jesus

In Hebrews chapter 10, we find that our Lord Jesus has opened a new and living way for us through the veil, that is, His flesh. So the veil in the tabernacle is a type of the flesh of our Lord Jesus. That is to say, this veil represents the earthly life of our Lord Jesus. The Word became flesh and tabernacled among man, full of grace and truth (see John 1:14).

When our Lord Jesus became a man upon this earth, His flesh is represented by the veil that separated the holiest of all from the holy place. What does that mean? Blue is the color of heaven. Purple is the color of wealth (In the old days, those wealthy people, they dressed in purple.) Scarlet is the color of royalty. Linen, in the Scripture, represents purity. So you find that the life of our Lord Jesus on earth is heavenly, is rich, is royal, and is pure.

A Pure Life—Linen

Can you ever find a life on earth so pure as the life of our Lord Jesus? He is like the fine linen. Everything about Him is pure, not only clean, but pure. You know, there is a difference between cleanness and pureness. Clean is without any defilement, but pure is singleness. The life of our Lord Jesus is such a pure life. His life is pure towards God; there is no opportunity for ulterior motive in Him. His whole life is governed by the Father's will—a life that is clean and pure. No one can point out any sin in Him. He challenged people saying, "Can you point out anything in me?" He is the sinless One. He has never committed any sin. He does not know what sin is, but He is more than that. He is pure. He always obeyed His Father. His heart is single towards His Father. His life on earth is like the twined byssus, the twined linen.

A Heavenly Life—Blue

And there you will find it is mixed with blue—heavenly. Even though He walked on earth, He is in heaven. He said, "No one has ever ascended to heaven, but He who has descended from heaven is yet in heaven" (see John 3:13). So our Lord Jesus, while He was on earth, He is a heavenly Man upon this earth. Wherever He goes, He brings with him a heavenly atmosphere. His touch is a heavenly touch. He is different. He is in the world, but He is not of the world because He belongs to heaven.

A Rich Life—Purple

And there you will find the riches of Him—purple. Even though He was born in a manger, even though He was born and reared in a carpenter's family, and yet He was so rich—the riches of His grace and the riches of truth in Him.

A Royal Life—Scarlet

Then of course, He was so royal—scarlet. Though He was humble, and yet He was so majestic. He was so royal. You can see the kingly manner in Him. He was in control over every situation. That was the life of our Lord Jesus. There was never a human life lived on earth like that of the Lord Jesus.

A Perfect Life—Cherubim

The cherubim were embroidered there all over the veil. The cherubim, so far as I understand it, represent the divine, original concept of God towards creation. In other words, before God created all things, He had an original concept about them—the pattern. He had an idea what creation should be, what the created beings should be. And these are represented by the cherubim.

So, here you find the cherubim were embroidered all over that veil. In other words, the life of our Lord Jesus answered completely to God's concept of what creation should be. He was *the* Man, the Man after God's own heart, the Man that God created for

Himself. Adam, the first man that was created, failed. And when he sinned, he was driven out of the Garden of Eden, and God set up cherubim to guard the way to the Tree of Life. In other words, God said, "You have fallen but My divine concept will never change. It still remains, and I will get what I am going to get." And you know, God got His Man in Christ Jesus. He is the Man. He was the veil.

A Holy Life—Separation

You know, the veil had two sides, and the inner side of the veil faced the mercy seat. In other words, so far as the Lord Himself was concerned, He lived such a life on earth that He was in constant communion with His Father. He saw His Father's face all the time. He pleased His Father all the time. And His Father said, "This is My beloved Son in whom I am well-pleased."

On the other hand, this veil separated everything outside the veil from the holiest of all. Only the Lord Jesus, as the Man after God's own heart, had the right and the privilege to dwell in God's presence. He was the only One who was worthy. He was the only One who could dwell in God's presence. Nobody else could because if anybody else dared to enter within the veil without the blood, he would be smitten to death.

God is holy. No one can see God who is not holy. And that is the reason why you find no one could enter behind the veil. Who could stand before the Holy God? Who could live in the presence of God? Nobody could. Therefore, the strange thing was that the life of our Lord Jesus was so perfect He was the only One who could live in the presence of God. But at the same time, He became the veil that separated us from God's presence.

Some people say, "We need to imitate Christ." Some people say, "Christ came into the world to set an example for us, and we should copy Him, follow Him." But do we know that the very life of Christ on earth, instead of saving us, actually condemns us? If Christ had not come, we do not have a perfect example of the life that pleases God. We have nothing to compare with us. But with the coming of Christ, we have a perfect example of the Man of God's heart. And dear brothers and sisters, will His life not condemn us instead of saving us? The more we see the life of our Lord Jesus, the more we are condemned because He is worthy, but we are not. He can see the Father's face, but we cannot. His life will condemn us.

The Rent Veil—a New and Living Way

He is the veil but thank God that veil was rent. Our Lord Jesus came into this world, not just to exhibit a perfect life to us. The Lord Jesus came to this earth in order to die. He was the perfect Man, the One who was sinless, but He was made sin for us that we might become the righteousness of God in Him (see II Corinthians 5:21). It is not the *life* of our Lord Jesus on earth that saves us. It is the *death* of our Lord Jesus on the cross that saves us.

Our Lord Jesus came into this world. He bore His cross all His life. The shadow of the cross cast over His whole life. And then finally, He was brought outside the city of Jerusalem to Golgotha, and there He was crucified. A marvelous thing happened. When Christ cried out with a loud voice, "It is finished," and He gave up His spirit to the Father in Golgotha, outside the city of Jerusalem, at that very moment, the heavy veil in the temple in Jerusalem was rent from top to bottom into two (see Matthew chapter 27). This veil that separated the holiest from the holy place was rent at the very moment when Christ died, and it was rent from top to bottom, not from bottom to top. In other words, it was not rent by human hands. God rent that veil. On Calvary's cross, God broke the body of Christ, and there in the temple, God rent the veil. And when the veil was rent, what happened? The way to the holiest was opened.

How we do praise and thank God that today the veil is rent! In other words, that which separates us from God has now been removed; therefore, Christ has opened a new and living way for us into the holiest of all. Do you know that before Christ died, no one could live in God's presence? But today, because Christ has died, the veil has been rent. There is no reason for us not to live in God's presence. A life within the veil is the right and the privilege of every believer today. Are you living there? In the past such a life was impossible, but now such a life is your portion. Why not live within the veil?

Many Christians today are still living in the outer court. Some Christians are living in the holy place. But remember, Christ has opened the new and living way for us to live in the very presence of God in the holiest of all. This is our portion.

In the outer court, people came to offer sacrifices. We may say, as believers, we do preach the gospel. We do help people, point people to Christ. It is like offering sacrifices on the brazen altar. This is our relationship with the world, but this is not the place where we live.

In the holy place, the priests serve. Now it is true, as the priests of God, we not only serve the world by preaching the gospel, helping people and pointing people to Christ, but we also serve God. In what sense? We light the lamp-stand. That is to say, we bear the testimony of Jesus. The church is like the lamp-stand that bears the light, and the light is Christ. So we bear the testimony of Jesus with our life. We tell people with our words. We tell people who Jesus is, what He is to us. This is our testimony. We also exhibit Christ like putting the shewbread on the table of shewbread. When we break the bread, when we drink the cup, we exhibit the death of Christ. We exhibit Him. We also burn the incense when we pray and when we worship. That is true.

In the outer court, to the world, we preach the gospel. In the holy place, in the church, we serve and worship God. But where do we live? We do not live in the outer court, nor do we live in the holy place. We should live in the holiest of all. And if we live in the holiest of all, then we can serve God in His church, and we can serve the world with the gospel. Otherwise, where do we have the power for it? So the question is, where do we live?

Brothers and sisters, do not think that to live a life within the veil is for a chosen few. If you know mysticism, then mystics will tell us this is a life for a chosen few only. If you are not among the chosen few, then this is not a life for you. But dear brothers and sisters, that is mysticism. That is not the Bible. What the Bible tells us is that this life within the veil is the right of every believer, every child of God. We do not need to live in the outer court, far away from God, engaged in all kinds of activities, but that is about all. Is our Christian life just activities? Very busy? Well, we should be busy. But is that all Christian life is? No. Or is it that our life is just that we come together to worship? Is that all? No. God's purpose is that we may dwell in His very presence, that we may see His face day by day, that we may behold His glory. It is the life within the veil that Christ has provided for us.

How can we go through this time of shaking when everything is being shaken around us? How can we go through this time if all our Christian life is just activities in the outer court? One day we may not be allowed to be active anymore. Then what will happen to us? If our Christian life is just that we come together to worship God, to exhibit Christ, thank God for that; we should do that. But there may be a time when we are not allowed to meet. Then what will happen? Will our Christian life collapse? Will it be wrecked?

In many places in the world, Christians have found this out: that their outward activities cannot save them. Even the so-called church life cannot save them. But there is one thing that is basic. Now I do not mean that we should not be active. We should. I do not mean that we should not have church life. We should. But there is something foundational: We must have a life within the veil, because one day all these things will be shaken away. But thank God, this life is ours! The veil is rent.

Many Christians today still seem to live before the veil, as if the veil has not been rent, as if the veil is still upon their face. They cannot see God. But remember this: The veil is rent. Christ has opened that new and living way for us and let us enter in.

The Life Within the Veil

What is meant by the life within the veil? Of course, in the Scripture, we find there are many different ways to describe this life within the veil. And remember, what is described is not for a select few. What is described actually is our common portion, our inheritance in Christ.

A Hidden Life

First of all, a life within the veil is a life hidden with Christ in God, and Christ is our life (see Colossians 3:3-4). Do we have a hidden life with Christ? Is our life just a life lived before man? In other words, is our life just a life lived in the outer court? People are there in the outer court, and we are seen. In the outer court we are busily engaged. We may be helping people to bind the sacrifice and then do all kinds of things. But do we have a life hidden with Christ in God? How much of that hidden life do we have?

Look at David. Before David was manifested to the nation of Israel, he had a hidden life, unknown to man, but known to God. Not even his family knew about it. While he was a shepherd tending the sheep, a lion came, a bear came, and under the anointing of God, how he smote the lion and the bear and delivered the sheep. It was something that happened to him, but he never broadcast it. Not even his father knew about it, not even his brethren knew about it. He had a hidden life with God.

How much of such a hidden life do we have? Is our Christian life just a life before man? Of course, there must be a life before man because that is our testimony. But do we have a hidden life with God? In our daily life, is our life hid with Christ in God? Is there something going on between us and God, unknown to man, but known to God? This is the kind of life within the veil, and that kind of life will become our power, the power of our testimony. And because it is a life hidden with Christ in God, therefore it is beyond the touch of the enemy.

The Bible says that we are seated with Christ in the heavenlies. He has not only quickened us out of death, He has not only raised us up from the dead together with Christ, but He has seated us with Christ in the heavenlies and that is to say, everything is under our feet. This is the life hidden with Christ in God. Do we have such a life? Remember, this is our right; Christ has opened it for us.

A Life of Making God Our Home

Now, what is this life behind the veil? It is a life that makes God our home. In Psalm 90, Moses said, "Lord, Thou hast been our dwelling place in all generations" (vs. 1). The word *dwelling place* means "home." In other words, Moses realized that God is His home. A life within the veil is a life at home with God. Do you take God as your home?

Well, the Scriptures sometimes say, "God is my refuge." Thank God for the refuge, but He is more than a refuge. You flee to a refuge when you are in trouble, but you go home because that is your home. Many Christians take God as their refuge. Thank God for that; He is your refuge. When you are in trouble, cry to Him, and He will answer you, and He will deliver you. Thank God for that! But that is not good enough. God is your home. That is where you dwell. He is your dwelling place; that is where you live.

And home is a place of rest. Therefore, in Hebrews, we find we have a rest that is promised to us, and this rest is none other but a life behind the veil. We rest in God. We rest from our own works. It is not a place of striving and struggling, but it is a place where we rest by faith in Christ Jesus.

Home is a place of love. We enjoy the love of God, and we love God.

Home is a place of satisfaction. We find satisfaction in God, and God finds His satisfaction in us. I like the word in Habakkuk. Even though everything around you may not be right, and yet he said, "God is my delight. I am satisfied in God." No matter how unsatisfying our environment may be, if we live a life behind the veil, we are satisfied in God. Make God your home. Stay there.

A Life of Abiding

A life within the veil is a life of abiding. In John chapter 15, the Lord said, "I am the true vine, and you are the branches. Abide in me, and I abide in you, and you will bear much fruit."

He is the true vine, and you are the branches. And you have a responsibility in you—abide in Him. Make your home in Him. Be in communication with him. Do not let your communication with Him be interrupted by anything. If there is any sin, confess it. If there is any disobedience, surrender. Let there be nothing interrupting your communion with Him. It is a picture of union and communion, the picture of the vine and the branches. It is a picture of union because the Lord said, "I am the vine, you are the branches." That is union. He does not say, I am the root of the vine, and you are the branches. He said, "I am the vine"—the whole vine—"and you are the branches." You are part of Me. That is union and because there is union there ought to be communion. The sap of the vine will flow into every branch. If there is no interruption, then naturally all these branches will bear much fruit. This is the life within the veil. There is union and communion, and out of that union and communion there is fruitfulness.

What is fruit? There is a difference between fruit and work. Work is something that you do, you put on with effort. Fruit is something that is produced out of the abundance and maturity of life. That is fruit. In a sense, it is effortless, unconscious, but to the glory of God. It is a life of abiding. You live in Him; you abide in Him.

A Life of Light

What is this life behind the veil? It is the life that is described by the apostle John in His first epistle. He said, "God is light. Walk in the light as He is in the light, and you have fellowship with one another, and the blood of Jesus Christ, God's Son, cleanses you from all your sins" (1:5-7).

God is light, and you walk in the light. The light here is not artificial light. In the outer court, you have the sunshine—created light. In the holy place, you have the light of the lamp-stand—artificial light. But in the holiest of all, you have the glory of God as light. In other words, God is light.

If we live a life within the veil, then God is light. He shines in us, and we walk in that light of life, we have fellowship with one another. And if there is anything wrong, the blood of Jesus Christ cleanses us from all sins. It is a life walking in the light of God.

A Life of Practical Righteousness

It is a life of practical righteousness. God is righteous. Therefore he that is born of God must practice righteousness—practical righteousness. In our daily life, we have to be right. And how can we be right? (Not that we can, but He can, who is our life.) If we let Him live, then we find we will practice righteousness as He is righteous (see I John 2:29).

A Life of Love

God is love. Therefore, let us love one another (see I John 4). Walk in love. How can we do that? If we live behind the veil, if we live before God, if we live by the life of Christ, then of course, His love in us will love out from us, and we will be able to love the brethren, love the unlovely. It is a life behind the veil.

The Law of the Spirit of Life

What is this life behind the veil? It is described in Romans chapter eight. The law of the Spirit of life sets us free from the law of sin and of death. Now this is the kind of life behind the veil. Because we are behind the veil, therefore the law of the Spirit of life functions; the law of the Spirit of life operates. And when the Spirit of life operates, it overcomes the law of sin and of death. The law of sin is: We do what we should not do. That is the law of sin. The law of death is: We cannot do what we should do. That is the law of death. And is it not true that oftentimes we feel we cannot do what we should do, and we do what we should not do? We are under the law of sin and of death. But thank God, if we live a life behind the veil, another law operates, a higher law operates—the law of the Spirit of life. In other words, life operates, and this life is resurrection life. It overcomes even death. It is a victorious life. It is a glorious life.

A Transforming Life

And what is this life behind the veil? Behind the veil with unveiled face, you behold the glory of God face to face. And there you will be transformed from glory to glory according to His image by the Lord the Spirit (see II Corinthians 3:18). It is a transforming life.

If you want to be transformed according to His image, you have to live a life behind the veil, because if you live before the veil, you will not see His face. And if you do not see Him, the Holy Spirit is not able to do the work of transformation. You have to see Him, and then He will put a desire within your heart to be like Him and the Holy Spirit will transform you from glory to glory according to His image.

So, dear brothers and sisters, this life within the veil is the only life that we must live. Do not think that we have some other kind of life we can choose to live. The Lord Jesus, through His death, the breaking of His body, has opened this new and living way for us.

What a price He has paid for us that we may, by Him, live within the veil in the very presence of God, beholding His glory day by day, and being transformed. What a redemption He has accomplished for us! Look at what He has done for us! And then He said, come in and live there.

This is the only life for us. There is no other life. Do not be content to live in the outer court. We may live in the outer court for a long time, but the shaking is coming. And if that is the place where we live, we will be shaken off. Do not even just live in the holy place. It is good, but the shaking is coming. Even that is not enough. The only life that we must live is the life that Christ has ordained through His suffering for us. It is a life within the veil.

Oh, if only we can see that this is a life that Christ has opened for us, and this is the only life that we must live, then we will not linger in the outer court, nor even stay long in the holy place, but we will live in the holiest of all. Yes, we will come out and serve in the holy place and serve in the outer court, but we live in the holiest of all—behind the veil.

So, in the book of Hebrews, we are told that the secret of passing through great shaking and remaining unshaken is to live behind the veil, within the veil.

That is the secret, and this is an open secret. It is open to everyone. So may the Lord help us.

3—Outside the Camp

Hebrews 12:25-29—See that ye refuse not him that speaks. For if those did not escape who had refused him who uttered the oracles on earth, much more we who turn away from him who does so from heaven: whose voice then shook the earth; but now he has promised, saying, Yet once will I shake not only the earth, but also the heaven. But this Yet once, signifies the removing of what is shaken, as being made, that what is not shaken may remain. Wherefore let us, receiving a kingdom not to be shaken, have grace, by which let us serve God acceptably with reverence and fear. For also our God is a consuming fire.

Hebrews 13:10-16—We have an altar of which they have no right to eat who serve the tabernacle; for of those beasts whose blood is carried as sacrifices for sin into the holy of holies by the high priest, of these the bodies are burned outside the camp. Wherefore also Jesus, that he might sanctify the people by his own blood, suffered without the gate: therefore let us go forth to him without the camp, bearing His reproach: for we have not here an abiding city, but we seek the

> coming one. By him therefore let us offer the sacrifice of praise continually to God, that is, the fruit of the lips confessing His name. But of doing good and communicating of your substance be not forgetful, for with such sacrifices God is well pleased.

The book of Hebrews is written to the Hebrew believers in the first century to prepare them for the shaking that was soon coming upon the world. We know that in AD 70, God allowed the city of Jerusalem and the temple in it to be completely destroyed. This was a great shaking to the Jewish people at that time. We cannot imagine what a great shaking it must have been to those people. And this was a great shaking to the Hebrew believers too because they tended to cling to Moses as they clung to Christ. But it is God's will that they should be completely freed from the bondage of Judaism into the perfect liberty of Christ. God wanted these people to make a break from Moses into His Son, the Lord Jesus, and this shaking was to serve such purpose. Through the destruction of Jerusalem and its temple, the Hebrew believers were finally being released from Judaism into Christ because this is the will of God.

Now brothers and sisters, we mention again and again that this book of Hebrews is most relevant to our days because we are also in a time of great shaking. I think everybody can see that we live in the hour of shaking. Not only earthly things are being shaken, but even heavenly or spiritual things are also being shaken. The reason why such shaking is taking place is that which can be shaken will be removed, so that that which cannot be shaken may remain. Anything that can be shaken shall be removed because God has given us a kingdom that cannot be shaken, and He wants us to inherit that kingdom.

When such shaking is happening around the world, people are just frightened to death as they think of the things that are coming. But the Bible says this is the time that we who are the Lord's, who have been forewarned and foretold, should raise up our heads for our redemption draws near (Luke 21:28).

God prepared the Hebrew believers of the first century for this great shaking. He gave them definite instructions by which they could stand through the time of shaking and stand before God. And we believe that the instruction given in this book is for us today.

We have mentioned that there are two phrases in this book that serve as guideposts for us. One is *within the veil*, that is, God wants us to live within the veil. This was a privilege that the people in the Old Testament time never had. Once a year, the high priest, by the blood and the smoke of the incense, entered into the holy of holies to make atonement for himself and for the people, and he had to retreat very quickly. The Holy Spirit indicated by this that the way to the holiest of all is not yet open.

But thank God, through the death of our Lord Jesus, the veil that separated the holiest from the holy was rent. When our Lord Jesus died on the cross, at the very moment when He cried with a loud voice, "It is finished," and He gave up His spirit to the Father, there within the city, in the temple, that veil was rent from top to bottom. And because of the rent veil, the way to the holiest is open to us. We may enter in, not only to enter in, but it is the will of God that we should dwell within the veil. To live within the veil is now our privilege. God does not want us merely to be active in the outer court, helping the people, preaching the gospel. This is what we will do, but God does not want us to live there. God does not want us to live in the holy place. There, as priests, we will serve God, testify of Him, worship Him, and pray to Him. But the outer court is not the place where we live. God wants us to dwell, to make our home, to live constantly and continuously in His presence within the veil because our life is hid with Christ in God. God is now our home. There we shall abide. There we shall gaze upon Him. We shall see the glory of the Lord and be transformed from glory to glory, according to His image, by the Lord, the Spirit.

So, how can we go through this time of great shaking and not be shaken off, but will be able to stand before God, holy and without blemish? The secret is that we must dwell within the veil. We must live day by day, hour by hour, moment by moment in the very presence of God. And this is something that our Lord Jesus has given to us. Again, let us say that it is not just for a privileged few. It is for every believer.

Now, we would like to continue on with the second guidepost: *outside the camp.* Within the veil and outside the camp are two related matters. In other words, if you live within the veil, then you will go outside the camp. To live within the veil is to live before God; to go outside the camp is to live before man. Within the veil speaks of our hidden life in God, unseen by man, but seen by God. Outside the camp is our life before the world as a witness and a testimony for God. The more we live within the veil, the more we will go out of the camp. The more we go out to Him, outside the camp, the more we will experience the closeness and the nearness of Him within the veil. These two things go together. Within the veil gives us the strength to go outside the camp. And to go outside the camp confirms that which we have seen and heard within the veil. So, it is not enough that we live within the veil, but if we do, then we must go forth to Him outside the camp.

What is the Camp?

First of all, we would like to mention what the camp is. If you read Hebrews chapter 13, you will find the phrase outside the camp or outside the gate, as if the camp and the city are one and the same thing. Now, in a sense, that is true. If you know the background, after the children of Israel were delivered out of Egypt, as they were traveling through the wilderness, they were as a camp, the camp of God. Because they were traveling, therefore they camped along the way. But after they arrived in the Promised Land, they dwelt in cities. And of course, the most well-known city is Jerusalem. So, as a matter of fact, the camp and the city are one and the same thing. It just shows that in the wilderness they camped; in the Promised Land they lived in the city.

What is the meaning of a camp or a city? A camp or a city speaks to us of a certain boundary, which is well organized into a unit. It is not scattered sands, but it is something that has been highly organized into a unit. A certain boundary is there, and that is what a camp or a city speaks to us. Generally speaking, the world today is a camp or a city.

The Secular World

In the beginning, God created the earth, and God gave the earth to man to live, to enjoy, and to rule for him. But unfortunately, man sinned against God, and through the fall of man, not only man fell under the rule of the archenemy of God and man— Satan—but through man, Satan was able to usurp the earth. He took the earth from the hand of mankind and organized it into a cosmos, a system; so the whole world today is a system. Whether it is political, or economic, or educational, or even religious, the whole world today is a world system, organized by Satan as a unit. He uses this world system to oppose God, to fight against God's purpose, to try to delay the coming of the kingdom of God. This is what the world is. It is a camp, a city, represented by Babylon. Once we belonged to the world; we were part of it. We were under the dominion of the wicked one. But thank God, He has delivered us! He has taken us out of the world and has given us to His son, our Lord Jesus.

In the World—Not of the World

What is our position today? We are *in* the world, but we are not *of* the world. Now, it is not the will of God that we should go out of the world today. I often think how good it would be if the moment you are saved you are raptured. That will save so many problems. But this is not God's will. Even though He has saved us, He has taken us out of the world and given us to Christ, and yet we are still in the world, physically speaking. But thank God, spiritually speaking, we are not *of* the world. We are *in* the world, but not *of* the world. Just as our Lord Jesus, when He was on earth, He was in the world, but He was not *of* the world. This is our position.

The Things of the World

We do not belong to this world system, even though we are still here, and because of this, we are exhorted not to love the world: "Love not the world or the things of the world, because if you love the world, then the love of the Father is not in you" (see I John 2:15).

What is the world? The world is presented to us in the form of things. The world has many things, beautiful things, attractive things. And the world offers these things to entice us and draw out from us the lust of the flesh, the lust of the eyes, and the pride of life.

God created this earth and all the things in it for man to enjoy. God created us with desires and needs. These desires and needs will be met by the things that He created upon the earth. There is nothing wrong with these desires or needs that He has created in man, nothing wrong with the things that He created upon this earth to supply the needs of man. But today you find the enemy has organized the world and is using the things of the world to draw out lusts from them.

What is lust? Lust is illegitimate desire. There is nothing wrong with desire. If you are hungry, you need to eat. There is nothing wrong with that. But when the desire is drawn to an inordinate, improper, illegitimate, out-of-bounds, then it becomes a lust. And the enemy uses the things of the world to draw out the lust of the flesh. We not only want to live, but we want to live luxuriously. We want to live to satisfy our sinful passions. Our eyes also are never satisfied with the things that we see. And we want to compare ourselves with our neighbors, and that is the pride of life.

Dear brothers and sisters, these are the things of the world, and if we fall into the trap, then we will pierce ourselves with many sorrows, and the love of the Father will not be in us.

Conformed to the World

The Bible exhorts us not to be conformed to the world. "Be not conformed to the world, but be transformed by the renewing of your mind to prove what is the good and acceptable and perfect will of God" (Romans 12:2).

In the original, the meaning of "be not conformed to the world" means that the world is like a mold. Do not try to squeeze yourself into that mold. Or to put it in more modern language, do not try to be fashionable. The world has a kind of mold, a kind of fashion. Maybe every spring or every winter you find the wind of fashion blows. Probably, it starts in Paris or in New York, I do not know. And then when that fashion begins to blow, it blows all over the world, and everybody wants to follow the fashion. In other words, you squeeze yourself into that mold.

Dear brothers and sisters, you are too big for that mold; you are too dignified for that mold. You are not to follow the world. The world is to follow you. Why should we squeeze ourselves into the mold of the world and try to be fashionable? Now, I do not mean that we should be so outdated as to be ancient or antique. We should be modern, but we should not try to be fashionable and squeeze ourselves into the mold of the world.

Friendship with the World

The Bible tells us, if we try to be friends with the world, the friendship of the world will make us enemies of God (see James 4:4).

We should not try to cultivate such friendship with the world as to compromise ourselves, because if we do, we become enemies of God. Go outside the camp. God has already delivered us out of this world. We do not belong to this world; do not try to go back and belong. If we do, we lose our testimony.

The Religious World

If you read the context of Hebrews, you find this secular world is not what the Holy Spirit is trying to define to us as what the camp is. The camp or the city in Hebrews, is not the secular world as such. It is as if, to the believers, the world as a cosmos should already be settled with us. We are not of the world. That is it. So the writer of the Hebrews or the Holy Spirit is not so much concerned with the world as a camp or a city. Rather, it is the religious world.

Let me read a few comments by others on this:

> The camp was not Rome with its heathenism but Jerusalem with its religion and its revelation from God. There, Jesus was rejected of the Jews because He condemned their self-righteousness and formality. It is not the irreligious but the religious world from which we must go out; that is, from everything that is not in harmony with His cross and its spirit of self-sacrifice. Let us go forth; not from one religious connection to another, which in time proves to have as much of the spirit of the camp. No, let us go forth unto Him to closer fellowship, to more entire conformity to Him, the cross-bearer, to His meek and patient and loving spirit. Let us not cast our reproach on those we

leave behind, but let us bear His reproach—Andrew Murray

How does this apply to us now? Many interpret it as those believers of any intelligence were justified in holding no fellowship with those assemblies of believers who have not as much light as themselves. This is certainly not the mind of Christ. It is good to leave idolatry, such as that of Rome, and every worldly system calling itself Christian, which is really only an association of unbelievers with which some believers are mixed-up—Robert Govett

The temple is the center of earthly, ritualistic, legalistic religion. This religion is in the city. It is the religion of the world, part of its system. But God is not in the city or its temple. When in Christ, He came to it, [that is, God came to it], He was cast out into the place of curse. All classes of the city combined to despise and reject Him—the religious leaders, priests and rabbis, the politicians, and the men of law, judges, police officers, learned scribes, and the common people—all joined in thrusting Him away. Neither the city nor the temple saw Him again. He is not there, and it is

vain to seek Him there. It is at Calvary He must be first met and Calvary, the place of reproach, the only drawing unto the kingdom, the house, the heart, the glory of God. In plain language, it means that he who wishes to have fellowship with God in His holy heaven must abandon every system of religion, that is of law, of ceremonies, of self-effort, of human devising, of secular authority, and must accept the reproach of dependence upon a fresh fellowship with, of obedience to the Redeemer who suffered without the gate.
—G.H. Lang

Judaism Became *the Camp*

The camp was Judaism at the time of Christ and at the time of the first century before the destruction of the temple. Judaism had its beginning, its origin from God. God gave to Moses, the Law, the priesthood, and the sacrifices. It had its beginning in God, but gradually, through the hands of man, it had become an "ism," an organized system. Instead of a revelation from above, it had become a tradition of man.

So at the time of Christ, Judaism was a religious system. At the top of that system was the high priest, and with him were the 70 members of the Sanhedrin, the governing body of Judaism. And then you have the Sadducees, the Pharisees, the scribes, and the rabbis. Judaism was highly organized at the time of Christ. The high priest, the Sanhedrin, the Pharisees, the scribes—these were the governing body of Judaism. They defined and explained everything in Judaism; they were the authority. They controlled not only the body but the conscience of the Jewish people. If anyone dared to contradict their interpretations and concepts, they were excommunicated, cast out of the commonwealth of Israel.

When Christ the Messiah came, they cast Him out because Christ did not fit in with their interpretation of prophecy, with their concept of the Messiah. They expected a political Messiah, a Messiah that would come and deliver them out of the iron hand of the Roman Empire and make them the head of the nations. Instead they found that this Jesus of Nazareth came and preached about love and forgiveness. He had no interest in overthrowing the Roman yoke, but He was interested in delivering people from the yoke of sin. He did not fit in with their concept. He did not fit in with their interpretation. He did not follow them. He did not belong to the system. He dared to challenge their system and their tradition. And because of this, they got rid of Him. "Away with Him! Away with Him! Crucify Him" (see John 19:15). There was no place for the Messiah. It/Judaism was a camp, and Christ was cast out of the camp. They brought Him outside of Jerusalem to the place called Golgotha, "the place of the skull," and there they crucified Him with two robbers.

They did not know that it was a fulfillment of prophecy. It was a fulfillment of the type shown in the Old Testament, on the Day of Atonement (see Leviticus 16). Now it is true that sacrifices were offered on the altar day after day—sin offerings, trespass offerings. But it was on the Day of Atonement that a bullock and a goat were offered, and the blood of the goat and the bullock were carried by the high priest behind the veil. The blood was sprinkled upon the mercy seat, and there the high priest would make atonement for himself and for the people once a year before God.

All the sacrifices, all the sin offerings that were offered day after day were for personal reasons. However, on the Day of Atonement, that sacrifice was offered for the atonement of the whole nation. The blood was brought behind the veil to the very presence of God to make atonement for himself and for the people. But you find the bodies of the sacrifice were not to be eaten by the priest or by those who made offerings, like with the peace offerings. They were not to be burned on the altar completely like the burnt offering. No. The bodies of the goat and the bullock were carried outside the camp, and there they were burned into ashes. The body was burned outside the camp. The blood was brought within the veil.

Here you will find how it was fulfilled in the life of our Lord Jesus. How they pushed Him out of the temple, out of the city, to that place outside the camp, a place of curse and reproach. There they crucified Him. His body was broken at Calvary, but thank God, the blood was brought behind the veil to atone for the sins of the world. In order to sanctify the people, He was crucified outside the gate.

Why must the bullock and the goat be burned outside the camp, while the blood was brought within the veil? Because the camp was unclean, was defiled. In Exodus chapter 32, when Moses was at the top of the mountain receiving the Ten Commandments, the children of Israel below in the plain, worshipped the golden calf. God sent Moses down, and when Moses saw the scene, he broke the two tablets of stone—the Law—because they have broken the Law. He ground the golden calf into powder, cast it upon the water, and ordered the children of Israel to drink of the water, that is, to drink of their own sin.

Then, you remember how Moses stood at the gate of the camp, and said, "Whoever is with the Lord, come to me." Only the tribe of Levi came out of the camp to join with Moses. And Moses ordered them to go into the camp from one gate to the other and slay everyone they met, whether men, women or children, their relatives or their neighbors, to sanctify themselves.

Then in chapter 33 of Exodus, something happened. Moses took his own tent, pitched it outside the camp, and called it the tent of meeting. Whenever people wanted to inquire of God, they went outside of the camp to the tent of meeting. And when Moses went out of the camp to the tent, the glory of the Lord, the pillar of cloud, descended upon it. The people saw it and they worshipped. Because the camp was so defiled, Moses had to remove his tent outside the camp, and God's glory came upon that tent.

Christ, in order to sanctify us, could not do this work within the camp. Judaism was supposed to prepare for the coming of the Messiah, and yet He was not received; it was defiled. So He had to do the work of redemption outside the gate. There—outside the camp—He was crucified in order to bring His blood into the very heaven, into the very presence of God to atone for the sins of the world. That is the reason why the Bible says, "Let us go forth outside the camp to Him." He is not in the camp. He is outside. Therefore, anyone who wants to seek Him has to go outside the camp to seek Him.

In the book of Acts, chapter seven, in the testimony that Stephen gave, you find he told the people the same thing. God is no longer there in Jerusalem in the temple. They had to go outside the camp to meet the Lord. Judaism as a camp has not only rejected Christ, but they have persecuted those who followed Christ.

Christianity Became *the Camp*

Dear brothers and sisters, how does it apply to us today? Christianity has its origin from heaven. It began as a living revelation. It is a living faith. It is like a mustard seed, the smallest of all seeds, but it has life.

So, this faith comes from above. When Peter acknowledged our Lord Jesus as the Christ, the Son of the living God, He said, "Peter, son of Jonah, you are blessed because this is revealed to you by my Father, who is in heaven." It is a living faith.

After the death, resurrection, and ascension of Christ, at the Day of Pentecost, the church had its beginning. In the 28th chapter of Acts, Paul was in Rome, the end of the world. In 30 years, the gospel was preached throughout the known world at that time. The Roman Empire used its military and political power to try to wipe out Christianity, but the Roman Empire was wiped out. Christ and His followers conquered not by sword, but by love.

The church of God should remain in this world as small and despised in the eyes of man. This mustard seed should grow; it should grow as a vegetable because this is the will of God. But unfortunately, starting from the fourth century, man's hand began to come in to organize the living faith and to organize the revelation from above. Gradually, they diminished the church into an institution, powerful in this world. It became a tradition instead of revelation, a system instead of living faith. This mustard seed had grown abnormally into a big tree, out of its kind, out of God's order, and all the birds of the air came and roosted upon it. And if you read the first parable in Matthew 13, you know these birds represent the wicked ones. Instead of becoming a habitation of the holy God, it has become the roosting place of all wickednesses.

In the beginning, Christianity was like three measures of meal to be offered to God as an oblation or a meal offering. But then in the parable you find a woman came and put leaven in it. And leaven in the Scripture speaks of wicked doctrines or wicked manners. And the leaven inflated the three measures of meal making it palatable to human taste, but unfit to be offered to God. Christianity has become just like Judaism. It had its beginning in heaven, in God, but now it has become an earthly, human, religious system. And what happened to the system? They pushed Christ out of the camp.

Christianity Persecuted

If you read church history, you will find that during the first three centuries, the world as a cosmos, as a system, opposed Christ and persecuted His followers. The Roman Empire persecuted Christians. If you want to read how Christians died, read *Foxe's Book of Martyrs*. There you find people like Polycarp and others who gave their life for Christ. How the Roman Empire tried to wipe out Christianity—burning them, casting them to the lions, killing them. But the blood of the martyrs becomes the seed of the gospel, and the gospel spread.

Christianity Persecutes

After the fourth century, Christianity became a religious system. And after it became a religious system, part of the world, what happened? It began to persecute those who wanted to follow the Lamb whithersoever He goes. It is no surprise for the world to persecute Christians, but for the religious Christian world to persecute Christians is surprising; yet it is a fact.

I would like to read what Andrew Murray said:

> There is perhaps no greater need in our day than that God should open the eyes of His people to the solemn truth that the so-called Christian world is the very same world that rejected Christ. We are to bear to it the same relation He did.

Strong words, but true words.

The Roman Catholic System

When you come to the sixth century of church history, the Roman Catholic system was firmly established. Do you want to know how the Roman Catholic system persecuted the true believers of Christ? Let me go through the history with you just a little bit. (If you want to read more, there are volumes and volumes written about it.)

The Paulicians

In the middle of the seventh century there were the Paulicians. (We do not know why they are called Paulicians, probably because they put much emphasis on the writings of Paul.) These people existed in the area of Mesopotamia. They had a particular respect for the authority of the Bible and advocated a life of simplicity. Were a devoted and earnest people and brought a strong witness against the unsavory practice of the Catholic church. Their enemies testified against them, but their lives testified of Christ. The Paulicians accepted no central authority to rule over the scattered assemblies, the local churches looked to God as their Head. They were built up and strengthened spiritually by teachers who moved from place to place to minister in their midst. Their spiritual unity lay in a life which they had in Christ. They were the people who wanted to follow the Lamb whithersoever He went.

But do you know what happened? Not only were the leaders killed, but in the middle of the ninth century, there was notorious persecution under the Empress Theodora. Within the space of five years, 100,000 persons met their death. The Catholic system used the world to kill these followers of Jesus because they did not belong to the camp.

The Bogomils

In the middle of the eighth century, there were the Bogomils who lived in the Balkan Peninsula. (Bogomils simply means "friends of God.") They preached love and grace from the Gospels and exhibited the Christian virtues in their lives. Instead of ornate church buildings with all the attendant trappings, meeting places were plain and void of bells, images, or altars, or the believers could most equally well meet within their own houses. The Scriptural truth of the priesthood of all believers was recognized; the congregation was governed by a plurality of elders and edified through the teaching of ministering brothers. The poor and needy among the church were also helped, according to the law of love in Christ.

The spread of these friends of God constituted an increasing threat to the Roman Church, and Rome was not inactive in seeking to stem the tide of its meek and powerful opposition. The king of Hungary was ordered to invade Bosnia, and the country was ravaged by a war that went on for years.

The Albigenses

Another illustration is in the 12th and 13th centuries; these were the Cathars, also known as the Albigenses. They fiercely denounced the prevailing ecclesiastical errors of the day and led people to a new life through the preaching of the Scripture.

The Waldensians

Also, there were the Waldensians. They were characterized by their marked reverence for the Scriptures, in which they found their rule of daily living and church rule. The knowledge of Christ dwelling within by the Spirit was to them the truth of paramount importance, but in matters of Scripture interpretation, which did not deny the basic necessity of this interpretation of Christ, they allowed a generous liberty. Salvation was through faith, and the Roman Church had authority neither to open nor to close the door to God's grace. The proof of salvation was holiness of life. Baptism was a testimony to faith in Christ, and the Lord's Supper was a remembrance of His sacrifice.

However, in 1348, under Charles IV, Emperor of the Holy Roman Empire, a determined effort was at once instituted to stamp out the Christian congregations. An Inquisition was brought into effect with diabolical efficiency. How that religious system, called Christian, persecuted those who belonged to Christ, who wanted to follow Christ all the way, because they did not belong to the camp!

The Protestant System

But do you think this is only happening with the Roman Catholic system? Thank God for the Reformation in the 16th century. Thank God for Luther, Calvin, Zwingli and these people through whom God has recovered justification by faith and the open Bible. But unfortunately, these Reformers did not go far enough. In other words, they came short of God. Even though they came out from under a Roman yoke, they came under the yoke of the different states or countries. In the beginning, it was a move of God, but then man came in and organized it and it became state churches—national religion.

Protestantism is no better than Catholicism. If you read church history, at the time of the Reformation, even the Reformers themselves, who were persecuted by the Roman Catholic system, they in turn, persecuted those who wanted to follow the Lord all the way. We know more about these things today than before because through research many hidden histories have been recovered.

The Anabaptists

The Anabaptists are an illustration. Actually, *Anabaptist* is a very general, vague term. It does not actually refer to any particular group, but Anabaptist simply means those who baptize again. Why? Because during the time of the Reformation, even people like Martin Luther still believed in infant baptism. But there were some people who were not involved in Catholicism, nor in Protestantism. They were free from the bondage of either, and they were able to go into the word of God in such simplicity that they began to see baptism is believers' baptism. In other words, they could not find infant baptism in the word of God, yet they were all baptized in the Roman system or in Protestant churches as infants. So when they began to follow the Lord and be baptized by water, they were called Anabaptists—those who baptize again, but in reality, they were being baptized for the first time.

These people refused to call themselves by any other name but Christians or brothers. They admitted baptism only to those who had an experience of regeneration through faith in Christ, but how they were persecuted, even by the Reformers. They were killed, burned, and hundreds were drowned. Their persecutors said, "Alright, you want to be baptized, we will baptize you." Then they tied a rock around their necks and drowned them—men, women, and children—hundreds and hundreds of them.

The Dissenters

This happened not only at the time of Reformation, but if you read on in church history, even in England, there was persecution. People who dissented, people who refused to take the oath of loyalty to the king (because the king was supposed to be the head of the church), were dissenters, non-conformists, and how they were persecuted. John Bunyan was imprisoned for 12 years and during that time he wrote *The Pilgrim's Progress* in prison.

The Moravians

Thank God, in the 18th century there was Count Zinzindorf. He opened his estate to receive those Moravians who were persecuted by the religious Christian world because of their faith. That was the beginning of the Moravian mission.

The Methodists

Think of John Wesley and George Whitefield. God used them, but they were not allowed to preach in so-called churches. So finally, they preached in the church graveyards.

This type of persecution of Christians by Christianity has continued on and on up to our time. How those true believers of Christ in China were persecuted more by the so-called Christian world than by the secular world. It is true that the Communist government persecuted them, but it is that so-called Christian organization, used by the Communists, that did the persecution.

There is no place for Christ in the camp. He is not there. And that is the reason why the word says, "Therefore, let us go forth to Him, without the camp."

If you want to follow the Lord, you have to go forth outside the camp to Him.

Life Outside the Camp

Brothers and sisters, we need to live within the veil, but at the same time, we have to go outside the camp. Why? What do we have outside the camp? If we read the Old Testament, we find that:

People who are cast outside the camp are the lepers—Leviticus 13.

People who are cast outside the camp to be killed are the blasphemers—Leviticus 24.

People who were cast outside the camp were the Sabbath breakers—Numbers 15.

Outside the camp is a place of curse and reproach, and that is the place that they cast our Christ into. Therefore, let us go forth to Him. The only attraction outside the camp is Him. Because He is there, where He is, there we need to be, bearing His reproach.

What kind of life is this life outside the camp?

A Life of Separation

First of all, it is a life of separation. We need to be separated from the world as a system, even if it is religious, because only through such separation are we able to join completely with the Lord. Separation and unity are not contradictory. Separation is unto unity. The Lord said, in John chapter 17: "You are not of the world. I sanctify Myself that they may be sanctified." Why? "That they may be one, as I and the Father are one." Today, if we are not separated from the world, we will not be able to be united into one. It is a life of separation.

A Life of Reproach

It is a life of reproach. It is the way of the cross. We have to bear His reproach. We have to take up the cross and follow Him. We will be misunderstood. We will be labeled. We will be accused, but this is where He is.

A Life of Faith

It is a life of faith because we do not have any abiding city here. We are looking for that city with foundations. We acknowledge ourselves as strangers, as sojourners, upon this earth. We do not expect anything on this earth, our expectation is in Him. It is a life of faith. We do not walk by sight, but by faith.

A Life of Worship

Thank God, it is a life of worship. Why? Because it is said, "By Him therefore, let us offer the sacrifice of praise continually to God" (Hebrews 13:15). Now, you would think that people in the camp, having everything, living such a comfortable, unchallenged life, and welcomed by everybody, certainly, they would be able to offer praises unto God. But strange to say, it is those who are outside the camp who are able to offer the sacrifice of praise.

What is the sacrifice of praise? A sacrifice costs you something; it hurts you in a sense. How many praises unto God are but lip service? There is no sacrifice involved. It is easy just to open your mouth and praise the Lord. It does not cost you anything. This is not the sacrifice of praise. The sacrifice of praise costs you something because you follow the Lamb withersoever He goes. Because you bear His reproach, it costs you something. And out of the sacrifice, praises ascend unto Him. That is the sacrifice of praise, and that kind of praise satisfies God's heart. Those who are outside the camp live a life of worship.

A Life of Giving

And another thing: "Of doing good and communicating of your substance be not forgetful, for with such sacrifices, God is well-pleased" (Hebrews 13:16). It is not those who live in prosperity, comfort, and popularity who give. No. Those who give are those who suffer. Oh, how the Macedonian believers gave! They gave, not out of their bounty, but out of their lack. Because they loved God so much, they gave themselves to God, and they wanted to have a part in the grace of giving. But with the Corinthians, you have to collect from them.

Brothers and sisters, those who are outside the camp are those who take care of the poor. They think of the needy and are willing to sacrifice themselves in order to satisfy and supply other people. This is the life we are expected to live.

In this day of great shaking, dear brothers and sisters, if we live within the veil and we go forth outside the camp, we will be kept by the Lord through the great shaking and be able to stand before His presence, holy and without blemish.

Our heavenly Father, we do thank Thee for giving us instructions, telling us how we should live in this time of great shaking. Our Father, we do pray that by the work of the Holy Spirit, we may be a people who live within the veil in heaven and go outside the camp here below. We ask Thee, Oh Lord, that these may be the characteristics of our life on earth, to the glory of Thy name. We ask in the name of our Lord Jesus. Amen.

TITLES AVAILABLE
from Christian Fellowship Publishers

By Watchman Nee

Aids to "Revelation"
Amazing Grace
Back to the Cross
A Balanced Christian Life
The Better Covenant
The Body of Christ: A Reality
The Character of God's Workman
Christ the Sum of All Things
The Church and the Work 3 Vols.
The Church in the Eternal Purpose of God
"Come, Lord Jesus"
The Communion of the Holy Spirit
The Finest of the Wheat – Vol. 1
The Finest of the Wheat – Vol. 2
From Faith to Faith
From Glory to Glory
Full of Grace and Truth – Vol. 1
Full of Grace and Truth – Vol. 2
Gleanings in the Fields of Boaz
The Glory of His Life
God's Plan and the Overcomers
God's Work
Gospel Dialogue
Grace Abounding
Grace for Grace
Heart to Heart Talks
Interpreting Matthew
Journeying towards the Spiritual
The King and the Kingdom
The Latent Power of the Soul
Let Us Pray
The Life That Wins
The Lord My Portion
The Messenger of the Cross
The Ministry of God's Word
My Spiritual Journey
The Mystery of Creation
Powerful According to God
Practical Issues of This Life
The Prayer Ministry of the Church
The Release of the Spirit
Revive Thy Work
The Salvation of the Soul
The Secret of Christian Living
Serve in Spirit
The Spirit of Judgment
The Spirit of the Gospel
The Spirit of Wisdom and Revelation
Spiritual Authority
Spiritual Discernment
Spiritual Exercise
Spiritual Knowledge
The Spiritual Man
Spiritual Reality or Obsession
Take Heed
The Testimony of God
The Universal Priesthood of Believers
Whom Shall I Send?
The Word of the Cross
Worship God
Ye Search the Scriptures

The Basic Lesson Series
Vol. 1 - A Living Sacrifice
Vol. 2 - The Good Confession
Vol. 3 - Assembling Together
Vol. 4 - Not I, But Christ
Vol. 5 - Do All to the Glory of God
Vol. 6 - Love One Another

TITLES AVAILABLE
from Christian Fellowship Publishers

By Stephen Kaung

Abiding in God
Acts
A Man in Christ (Traditional Chinese/Simplified Chinese)
"But We See Jesus"
The Charge to the Church
Concerning Spirituals – Vol. 1
Concerning Spirituals – Vol. 2
David
Discipled to Christ
Elijah and Elisha
Glory — As Seen by Ezekiel
God's Purpose for the Family
Government and Ministry
in the Local Church
The Gymnasium of Christ
Haggai
A House of Prayer
In the Footsteps of Christ
In Times of Shaking
I Corinthians — Called into Fellowship
II Corinthians — A Man in Christ
Isaiah—The Redemption of the Lord
The Key to "Revelation" – Vol. 1
The Key to "Revelation" – Vol. 2
Malachi (English / Traditional Chinese / Simplified Chinese)
The Master's Training
Men After God's Own Heart
Ministering the Word of God
Moses, the Servant of God
Nehemiah
New Covenant Living & Ministry
Now We See the Church
Proverbs
Recovery
Seven Visions of Christ in the Book of Revelation
Shepherding
Teach Us to Pray
The Songs of Degrees
The Sons of Korah
The Splendor of His Ways
Titus
Worship
Zechariah

The "God Has Spoken" Series
Seeing Christ in the Old Testament, Part One
Seeing Christ in the Old Testament, Part Two
Seeing Christ in the New Testament

ORDER FROM: 11515 Allecingie Parkway Richmond, VA 23235
www.c-f-p.com

www.ingramcontent.com/pod-product-compliance
Lightning Source LLC
LaVergne TN
LVHW020038100726
843051LV00024B/349

* 9 7 8 1 6 8 0 6 2 2 0 3 4 *